THE OFFICIAL
WEST HAM UNITED
FOOTBALL CLUB ANNUAL
2012

Written by Rob Pritchard
Design by Nicky Regan

A Grange Publication

© 2011. Published by Grange Communications Ltd., Edinburgh, under licence from West Ham United Football Club.

Printed in the EU.

Photography © West Ham United Football Club

ISBN: 978-1-908221-39-1

£7.99

2012

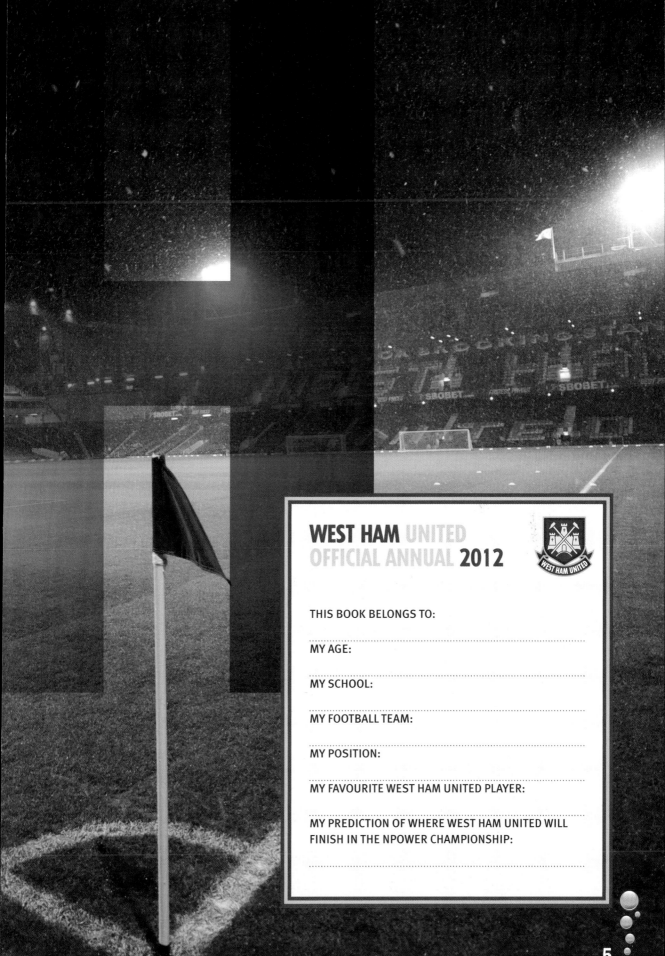

WEST HAM UNITED
OFFICIAL ANNUAL 2012

THIS BOOK BELONGS TO:

....

MY AGE:

....

MY SCHOOL:

....

MY FOOTBALL TEAM:

....

MY POSITION:

....

MY FAVOURITE WEST HAM UNITED PLAYER:

....

MY PREDICTION OF WHERE WEST HAM UNITED WILL
FINISH IN THE NPOWER CHAMPIONSHIP:

....

CONTENTS

INSIDE YOUR 2012
WEST HAM UNITED OFFICIAL ANNUAL

16

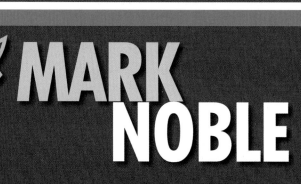

MARK NOBLE

Fans are the lifeblood of this football club and it is great to see you supporting us with passion and pride.

In the same way that the first team needs the Academy players coming through every year, so the club needs its young supporters to turn into loyal followers of the team home and away.

Wherever I have managed, I have always looked to develop homegrown players. We all know what it means to see local lads like James Tomkins or Freddie Sears come through and we want to keep this going.

A big draw for me coming to this club was the fantastic heritage and history of the greats like Bobby Moore and Trevor Brooking. I was fortunate to play against them in my early days as a player and it is right that we acknowledge the great names of the past while pushing this club forward.

There is nowhere with a better reputation than our Academy for churning out the talent of tomorrow. My coaches and I will work closely with Academy Director Tony Carr and his staff to make sure those who are doing well are given a chance to shine and know that we are impressed with their progress.

Everything we do at West Ham United is for the fans. We look to entertain and win every time we play and there is no doubt the tremendous backing you provide gives us a massive lift in the matches.

We will never take your support for granted and the players will make sure that they reward your support with 100 per cent effort and commitment.

This is a club with a great history and traditions and, I hope, a great future.

Up the Hammers!
Big Sam

2012

WELCOME FROM THE MANAGER

HAMMER
OF THE YEAR

Scott Parker completed a memorable personal hat-trick when he was voted Hammer of the Year for the third consecutive season.

The midfielder enjoyed an outstanding 2010/11 campaign, making 40 appearances and netting a career-high seven goals in all competitions.

Parker's efforts were appreciated by the supporters, who nominated him as their player of the year ahead of Robert Green and Mark Noble, while his team-mates also voted him as their Players' Player of the Year by an overwhelming margin.

For the player himself, the joy of winning two such prestigious awards was only marred by the Hammers' relegation from the Barclays Premier League.

"It's obviously a massive achievement for me and one I'm very proud of, but if I could have handed back all the personal accolades and awards I've got this season to have kept West Ham in the Premier League, then I would have," he said, with typical modesty.

"I think it is consistency, playing games and confidence that helped me to win the awards. I think it's a combination of things really, plus experience. I'm older now and I think that has led me to perform the way I've been performing really."

"We've got a young squad and when you see yourself as one of the older pros, you take that role up and that's what I've done. I'm a senior player and an older player so I've taken up that mantle along with some of the other players, so it's been OK."

Parker's form saw him recalled to the England team after a four-and-a-half year absence, and he took the opportunity with both feet by starring in victories over Denmark and Wales in 2011.

"It was massive for me to get back into the England team. As a kid you always want to play for England and that's what you want to do. My England career has probably been a bit stop-start, but I like to think I've been given a chance now and I've put my foot in the door a little bit.

"I'm certainly going to have to continue working hard because there are a lot of players in my position who are worthy of a place. It's going to be difficult but I'm going to try to keep my place."

The ever-popular Parker also picked up the Goal of the Season trophy for his outstanding strike against Liverpool in February 2011.

However, he was not the only winner at the club's third annual End of Season Gala Dinner, which was held in the Great Room at London's Grosvenor House Hotel in Park Lane.

The Young Hammer of the Year trophy went to Freddie Sears, while Australia Under-17 striker Dylan Tombides was rewarded for his efforts with the Academy Player of the Year award.

Carlton Cole picked up the Top Goalscorer award for the third consecutive season. Green grabbed the Save of the Season award for his outstanding stop from Tottenham Hotspur's Gareth Bale in March 2011, with Lars Jacobsen collecting the trophy on his behalf while the goalkeeper attended the birth of his first child.

Jonathan Spector nabbed the Individual Performance of the Season award for his two-goal display in the 4-0 Carling Cup victory over Manchester United in November 2010, while Victor Obinna received the Best Team Performance gong on behalf of the squad for their performance in the same fixture.

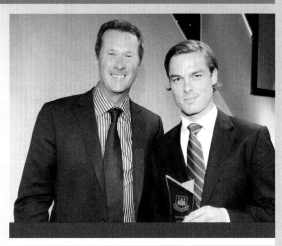

Award winners (clockwise from top left): Freddie Sears, Victor Obinna, Jonathan Spector, Scott Parker, Dylan Tombides and Hammer of the Year Scott Parker.

SHOW
YOUR
TRUE COLOURS

Can you fill in the missing colours on West Ham United's official club crest to show you are claret and blue through and through?

Can you spot the ten differences between the two images from West Ham United's npower Championship fixture against Cardiff City in August 2011?

Answers on page 58.

SPOT THE DIFFERENCE

Born in Dudley in the West Midlands in June 1954, Sam Allardyce is one of the most respected managers in English football.

An uncompromising defender in his playing days, Allardyce made more than 400 appearances for nine professional clubs in England, the United States and Republic of Ireland – most notably for Bolton Wanderers and Preston North End.

As a player, the centre-back won the Division Two title with Bolton in 1977/78 and was promoted from Division Four with Preston in 1986/87.

It is as a manager that Allardyce has made his name, however.

Known fondly throughout the game as 'Big Sam', he spent two years as assistant manager at West Bromwich Albion before taking his first No1 job as player/manager of League of Ireland side Limerick in 1991 – securing promotion to League of Ireland Division One in his sole season in charge.

On his return to England, Allardyce honed his managerial skills in the lower divisions with Preston,

Blackpool and Notts County, leading the latter to the Division Three title in 1997/98.

The Hammers boss is best known for his eight-year spell in charge at Bolton, leading The Trotters into the Premier League, the League Cup final and guided them into the UEFA Cup for the first time in the club's history.

During his time at the Reebok Stadium, Allardyce forged a reputation for introducing an innovative new training regime based on sport science and injury prevention, while he also attracted a host of overseas stars to the club.

After a successful eight years in Lancashire, he moved to Newcastle United in May 2007, spending six months at St James' Park before returning to the Red Rose County with Blackburn Rovers in December 2008.

Again, Allardyce impressed, leading Rovers to the League Cup semi-finals and a tenth-place Premier League finish in 2009/10 before leaving Ewood Park in December 2010.

Widely praised for his managerial and coaching skills, Allardyce joined West Ham United in June 2011 and will hope to enjoy similar success in east London.

MEET THE MANAGER
SAM ALLARDYCE

Neil McDonald
Assistant Manager

Wally Downes
First-team Coach

Born in the same town, Wallsend, as former West Ham United midfielder Michael Carrick, Neil McDonald was a reliable full-back who enjoyed success with Newcastle United and Everton. Capped five times by England at Under-21 level, McDonald featured for The Toffees in the 1989 FA Cup final before acting as Sam Allardyce's No2 at Bolton Wanderers and Blackburn Rovers.

Born in Hammersmith in west London, Wally Downes made his name as a member of the infamous 'Crazy Gang' during nine seasons as a professional with Wimbledon. The former midfielder, who turned 50 in June, embarked on his coaching career with Crystal Palace and Reading, where he worked under Steve Coppell, before joining West Ham United in November 2010.

Martyn Margetson
Goalkeeper Coach

Ian Hendon
Development Coach

A former Wales international goalkeeper, Martyn Margetson enjoyed a successful 15-year playing career with Manchester City, Southend United, Huddersfield Town and Cardiff City. The West Neath-born stopper became The Bluebirds' goalkeeper coach while still a player in 2005 before taking the role up full-time. He became Wales' goalkeeper coach in January 2011.

An experienced defender who played for Tottenham Hotspur, Leyton Orient, Sheffield Wednesday and Barnet during a 20-year playing career, Ian Hendon joined West Ham United as development coach in July 2011. A former England Under-21 international, Hendon won the FA Youth Cup during his time with Spurs and later managed Barnet for 18 months.

MEET THE BACKROOM STAFF

MEET THE SQUAD

The players who are aiming to fire West Ham United back into the Premier League in 2011/12.

West Ham United manager Sam Allardyce has put together a strong and experienced squad to challenge for promotion from the npower Championship this season. The Hammers' 2011/12 pool of players includes full internationals, experienced Premier League performers and a host of promising youngsters, all of whom have a single goal in mind.

Over the next nine pages, you will be introduced to the players who will be doing their best in claret and blue this term.

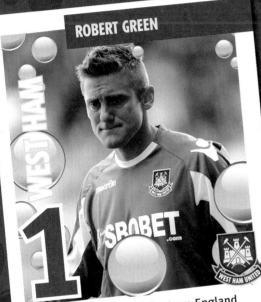

ROBERT GREEN

BORN: 18 January 1980, Chertsey, England
FORMER CLUBS: Norwich City

England international goalkeeper Robert Green has become a popular figure at the Boleyn Ground since joining West Ham United from Norwich City in August 2006.

A fine shot-stopper, Green has become the club's undisputed No1 in recent seasons, while also becoming a regular member of the senior England squad and appearing for his country at the 2010 FIFA World Cup in South Africa.

Voted Hammer of the Year for the 2007/08 season, the goalkeeper has also finished as runner-up for the prestigious award on two occasions.

A tall and powerful defender, Winston Reid started all three of New Zealand's matches at the 2010 FIFA World Cup in South Africa, scoring in the All Whites' 1-1 draw with Slovakia.

Comfortable at right-back or centre-back, Reid moved to Denmark at the age of ten, representing the Scandinavian nation at U19, U20 and U21 levels before switching international allegiance to the country of his birth in early 2010.

After five years of first-team action at FC Midtjylland in Denmark, the 6'3" player moved to West Ham United in August 2010.

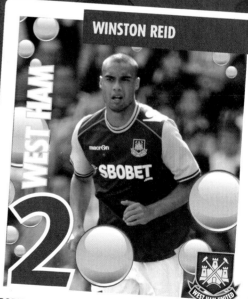

WINSTON REID

BORN: 3 July 1988, North Shore, New Zealand
FORMER CLUBS: SUB Sonderborg, FC Midtjylland

MEET THE SQUAD

George McCartney is an experienced Northern Ireland international left-back now in his second spell with West Ham United after joining the club on a season-long loan from Sunderland.

The Belfast-born defender initially moved to English football at the age of 16 with the Black Cats before moving to the Boleyn Ground in summer 2006.

After playing his part in the great escape from relegation in 2006/07, McCartney came runner-up in the Hammer of the Year award voting the following season before returning to Wearside.

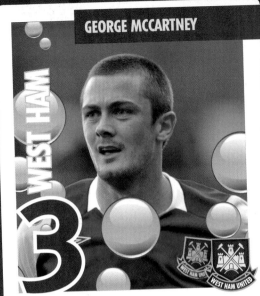

GEORGE MCCARTNEY

WEST HAM

3

BORN: 29 April 1981, Belfast, Northern Ireland
FORMER CLUBS: Sunderland, West Ham United, Sunderland, Leeds United (loan)

KEVIN NOLAN

WEST HAM

4

BORN: 29 March 1989, Basildon, Essex
FORMER CLUBS: Former clubs: Derby County (loan)

A goal-scoring midfielder, leader and inspirational figure, Kevin Nolan has enjoyed huge success with Bolton Wanderers and Newcastle United during his playing career.

Born in Liverpool, Nolan spent a decade in the first-team squad at Bolton, scoring exactly 50 goals in 345 appearances and regularly being tipped for full international honours.

Nolan maintained his consistency during a two-and-a-half year spell at Newcastle, where he captained the Magpies to the Championship title in 2009/10, before moving to West Ham United in July 2011.

A hugely-promising centre-back, James Tomkins became a regular member of the West Ham United first team during the 2009/10 season, making more than 25 appearances.

The ball-playing defender has been with the club since the age of seven and has long been considered one of English football's finest prospects.

That promise has been recognised at international level, with Tomkins graduating to England's Under-21 side and travelled to both the 2009 and 2011 UEFA European U21 Championship finals.

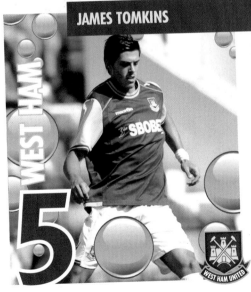

JAMES TOMKINS

WEST HAM

5

BORN: 24 June 1982, Liverpool, England
FORMER CLUBS: Bolton Wanderers, Newcastle United

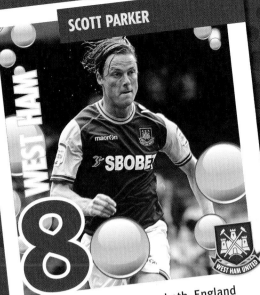

SCOTT PARKER

8

BORN: 13 October 1980, Lambeth, England
FORMER CLUBS: Charlton Athletic, Norwich City
(loan), Chelsea, Newcastle United

The outstanding Scott Parker has been a revelation since joining West Ham United from Newcastle United in the summer of 2007.

Parker's never-say-die attitude and driving midfield play have seen him voted Hammer of the Year for three straight seasons by the club's supporters.

The south London-born player's approach and impressive play have also earned him recognition by England and senior level, earning him a re-call to the international set-up in early 2011 after more than three years out of the picture.

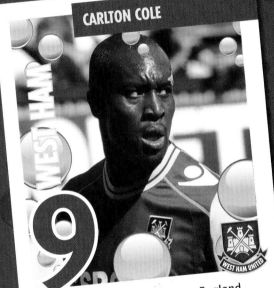

CARLTON COLE

9

BORN: 12 October 1983, Croydon, England
FORMER CLUBS: Chelsea, Wolverhampton Wanderers (loan), Aston Villa (loan), Charlton Athletic (loan)

Capped by England at full international level, Carlton Cole's career has flourished during his time at West Ham United.

A tall and powerful forward, Cole came through the ranks at Chelsea before finding his first-team opportunities limited by the arrival of a number of big-money signings at Stamford Bridge.

A popular character on and off the pitch, Cole is also heavily involved in charity and community work with a number of organisations.

JACK COLLISON

10

BORN: 2 October 1988, Watford, England
FORMER CLUBS: Peterborough United,
Cambridge United

A full Wales international at the age of 19, Jack Collison's career has flourished since he joined West Ham United as a 16-year-old scholar in the summer of 2005.

Already an important member of the Hammers squad, the all-action midfielder can contribute at both ends of the pitch.

While a serious knee injury has slowed Collison's progress somewhat, the youngster has the application and ability to reach the very top of the game.

JOHN CAREW

WEST HAM

11

BORN: 5 September 1979, Lorenskog, Norway
FORMER CLUBS: Lorenskog IF, Valerenga IF, Rosenborg BK, Valencia CF, AS Roma (loan), Besiktas, Olympique Lyonnais, Aston Villa, Stoke City (loan)

John Carew is a tall, skilful and vastly-experienced Norway international striker who has scored goals wherever he has played.

Carew has played professionally in Norway, Spain, Italy, Turkey, Italy and England since leaving his hometown club for Oslo-based Valerenga IF in 1998.

The Lorenskog-born forward joined West Ham United on 6 August 2011 following his release by Aston Villa, but still has plenty left to offer.

Mexico winger Pablo Barrera is widely considered to be one of the most exciting prospects in world football.

Two-footed, quick as lightning and blessed with the ability to go past his opponent with ease, Barrera made his name playing for Mexican side UNAM Pumas, where he won the league title in 2009.

Already capped more than 30 times at senior international level, Barrera helped his country to win the 2011 CONCACAF Gold Cup.

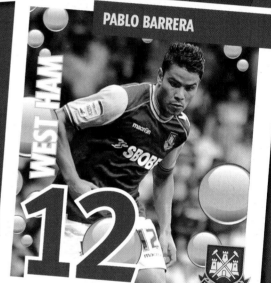

PABLO BARRERA

WEST HAM

12

BORN: 21 June 1987, Tlalnepantla, Mexico
FORMER CLUBS: Club Universidad Nacional (Pumas de la UNAM)

MATT TAYLOR

WEST HAM

14

BORN: 27 November 1981, Oxford, England
FORMER CLUBS: Luton Town, Portsmouth, Bolton Wanderers

A speedy and direct left-sided midfielder blessed with outstanding delivery and an eye for scoring truly spectacular goals, Matt Taylor joined West Ham United from Bolton Wanderers in July 2011.

A star as a youngster with Luton Town, Portsmouth and the England Under-21 side, Taylor has been a regular feature on Match of the Day for his penchant for smashing the ball into the net from all over the pitch.

Quick, elusive and always involved in the game, the Oxford-born wideman also featured in European competition during his time with Bolton Wanderers.

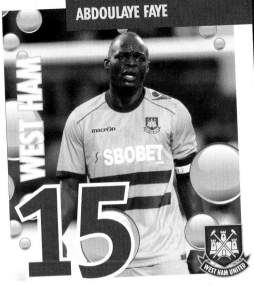

ABDOULAYE FAYE

15

BORN: 26 February 1978, Dakar, Senegal
FORMER CLUBS: ASEC Ndiambour, ASC Jeanne d'Arc, RC Lens, Istres (loan), Bolton Wanderers, Newcastle United, Stoke City

A powerful and experienced centre-back, Abdoulaye Faye joined West Ham United on a free transfer on 1 July 2011 following the expiry of his contract at Stoke City.

Capped more than 30 times by Senegal, Faye made his name in French football before initially moving to England with Sam Allardyce's Bolton Wanderers in the summer of 2005.

Respected for his committed approach and penchant for scoring important goals, Faye helped Stoke to reach the 2011 FA Cup final, having been voted Potters' Player of the Year in 2008/09.

Mark Noble ended the 2009/10 season as West Ham United's longest-serving player, having joined the club as a full-time trainee in the summer of 2003.

An experienced former England Under-21 midfielder, Noble has been part of the Hammers' promotion from the Championship and 'Great Escape' from relegation from the Premier League in May 2007.

After scoring on his 100th appearance for the club at Blackburn Rovers in March 2009, Noble has continued to be an important member of the first-team squad.

MARK NOBLE

16

BORN: 8 May 1987, Canning Town, England
FORMER CLUBS: Ipswich Town (loan), Hull City (loan)

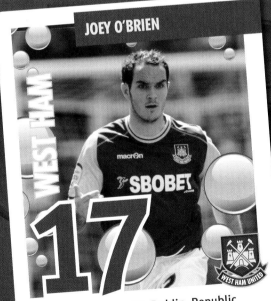

JOEY O'BRIEN

17

BORN: 17 February 1986, Dublin, Republic of Ireland
FORMER CLUBS: Bolton Wanderers, Sheffield Wednesday (loan)

Republic of Ireland international Joey O'Brien joined West Ham United on a free transfer following a successful week-long trial in July 2011.

A Premier League regular for Bolton Wanderers as a teenager, the Dubliner made his senior international debut just a week past his 20th birthday in March 2006.

Having suffered a disappointing three seasons fighting a succession of knee injuries, O'Brien proved his fitness to manager Sam Allardyce before being snapped up by the Hammers.

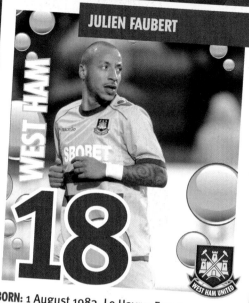

JULIEN FAUBERT

WEST HAM

18

The speedy France international right-back enjoyed a superb 2009/10 season, impressing West Ham United supporters with his outstanding attitude and commitment.

Faubert capped a fine campaign with a superb goal and all-round performance in the home Barclays Premier League win over Hull City in February 2010 – a display which earned him the Individual Performance of the Season award.

Faubert has filled in as a wide midfielder or even on the right of a front three at both first and reserve-team level.

BORN: 1 August 1983, Le Havre, France
FORMER CLUBS: AS Cannes, FC Girondins de Bordeaux, Real Madrid CF (loan)

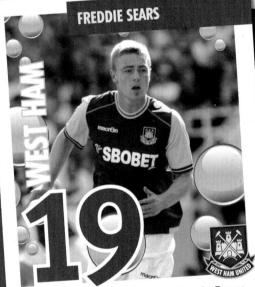

FREDDIE SEARS

WEST HAM

19

A lively striker who has come through the ranks at the Academy of Football, Freddie Sears has had a keen eye for goal since he was a young child.

A lifelong West Ham United supporter, Sears shot to the nation's attention when he scored on his Premier League debut against Blackburn Rovers in March 2008.

Sears' talents have also been recognised at international level, where he has already represented and scored for England at Under-21 level.

BORN: 27 November 1989, Hornchurch, Essex
FORMER CLUBS: Crystal Palace (loan)

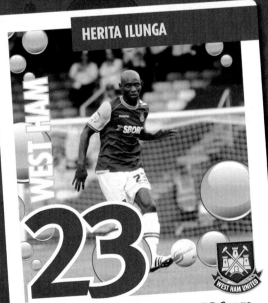

HERITA ILUNGA

WEST HAM

23

A buccaneering left-back who is both a strong attacker and a relentless, uncompromising defender, Herita Ilunga quickly settled into life at West Ham United following his arrival in summer 2008.

A DR Congo international with extensive experience in both the French league and in European football, Ilunga showed his talents during an explosive first season in the Premier League.

Although a series of injuries slowed the African during his second and third campaigns with the Hammers, there is no doubting Ilunga's pedigree.

BORN: 25 February 1982, Kinshasa, DR Congo
FORMER CLUBS: Amiens SC, Stade Rennais, RCD Espanyol, AS Saint-Etienne, Toulouse

A powerful and speedy forward, Frank Nouble joined West Ham United at the age of 17 in the summer of 2009.

The talented England Under-19 international scored on his Hammers debut in a pre-season win at non-league Thurrock on 24 July.

A fine full Barclays Premier League debut followed at Aston Villa in January 2010 before the striker headed off on productive loan spells at West Bromwich Albion, Swindon Town, Swansea City, Barnsley and Charlton Athletic.

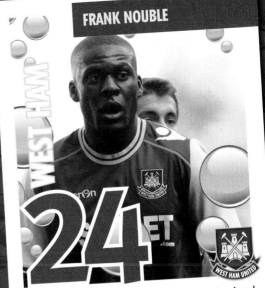

FRANK NOUBLE

BORN: 24 September 1991, Lewisham, England
FORMER CLUBS: Chelsea, West Bromwich Albion (loan), Swindon Town (loan), Swansea City (loan), Barnsley (loan), Charlton Athletic (loan)

JUNIOR STANISLAS

BORN: 26 November 1989, Kidbrooke, England
FORMER CLUBS: Southend United (loan)

A direct wide player who can also operate in a central forward role, Junior Stanislas is yet another talented young player to have come through the ranks at the Academy of Football.

Having caught the eye during two FA Cup meetings with Chelsea during a loan spell at Southend United, Stanislas broke into the West Ham United first-team at the end of the 2008/09 season.

The 2009/10 campaign saw the south London-born player continue with his development, netting important Boleyn Ground goals in the Carling Cup meeting with Millwall and Barclays Premier League draw with Fulham.

MAREK STECH

WEST HAM

29

Tall and confident, Marek Stech is one of a host of promising young goalkeepers at West Ham United.

Already capped by Czech Republic at Under-21 level, Stech was one of the hottest young properties in Europe when the Hammers secured his signature in the summer of 2006.

Having enjoyed loan spells at Wycombe Wanderers and AFC Bournemouth, Stech is ready to challenge the club's senior goalkeepers, including close friend Peter Kurucz, for a regular place in the first-team squad.

BORN: 28 January 1990, Prague, Czech Republic
FORMER CLUBS: AC Sparta Prague, Wycombe Wanderers (loan), AFC Bournemouth (loan) Stoke City (loan)

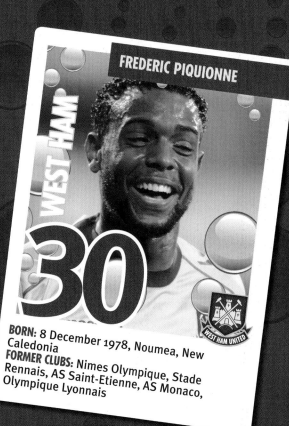

FREDERIC PIQUIONNE

WEST HAM

30

BORN: 8 December 1978, Noumea, New Caledonia
FORMER CLUBS: Nimes Olympique, Stade Rennais, AS Saint-Etienne, AS Monaco, Olympique Lyonnais

A tall and powerful forward, Frederic Piquionne became West Ham United's third summer 2010 signing when he arrived from French club Olympique Lyonnais.

Born on the Pacific Ocean collective of New Caledonia, Piquionne moved to the Caribbean nation of Martinique before settling into life as a professional footballer in mainland France in 2000.

On moving to England in 2009, France international Piquionne helped Portsmouth to reach their second FA Cup final in the space of three seasons.

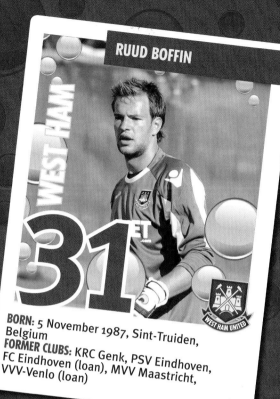

RUUD BOFFIN

WEST HAM

31

BORN: 5 November 1987, Sint-Truiden, Belgium
FORMER CLUBS: KRC Genk, PSV Eindhoven, FC Eindhoven (loan), MVV Maastricht, VVV-Venlo (loan)

A tall, blond goalkeeper, Ruud Boffin began his career with KRC Genk in his home country of Belgium before moving across the border to join Dutch giants PSV Eindhoven at the age of 17.

Boffin was loaned out to Eerste divisie club FC Eindhoven for a season before joining MVV Maastricht on a permanent basis.

Having arrived at West Ham United in summer 2010, Boffin made his first-team debut in a 1-1 Premier League draw at Blackburn Rovers in December of that year.

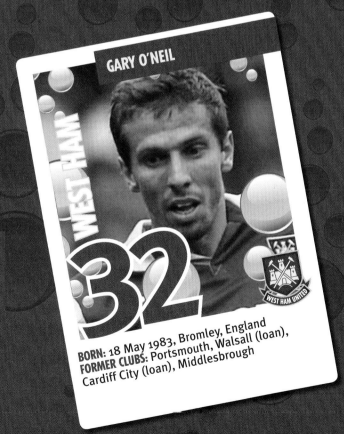

GARY O'NEIL

WEST HAM

32

BORN: 18 May 1983, Bromley, England
FORMER CLUBS: Portsmouth, Walsall (loan), Cardiff City (loan), Middlesbrough

A versatile and all-action midfield player capable of filling a variety of positions, Gary O'Neil joined West Ham United on a two-and-a-half year contract from Middlesbrough on 25 January 2011.

After starting his career with Portsmouth, O'Neil made more than 200 appearances for Pompey before joining Middlesbrough for a reported £5m on 31 August 2007.

The former England Under-21 international spent three-and-a-half seasons at the Riverside Stadium before moving to east London for an undisclosed fee.

1   West Ham United have won one major European trophy, lifting the European Cup Winners' Cup by defeating German side TSV 1860 Munich 2-0 at Wembley on 19 May 1965.

2   West Ham United are one of only two teams to score three goals in an FA Cup final and lose. The Hammers drew 3-3 with Liverpool in 2006 before being beaten on penalties. Bolton Wanderers are the other side to do so, losing 4-3 to Blackpool in 1953.

3   West Ham United are one of three clubs to appear in two League Cup finals and lose them both. Bolton Wanderers and Everton are the other two.

4   West Ham United have played at four different stadia since the club's inception in 1895 – Hermit Road in Canning Town, Browning Road in East Ham, the Memorial Grounds in Plaistow and the Boleyn Ground in Upton Park.

5   West Ham United have been involved in three 5-5 draws in their history – at home to Aston Villa on 3 January 1931, at Newcastle United on 10 December 1960 and at Chelsea on 17 December 1966.

6   Bobby Moore's No6 shirt was retired in August 2008 to mark the 50th anniversary of the England great's West Ham United debut against Manchester United on 8 September 1958.

9   West Ham United's longest winning streak of league matches was the nine victories they recorded from 19 October and 14 December 1985.

10   West Ham United hold the record for the joint-biggest victory in the League Cup. The Hammers defeated Bury 10-0 in the second round on 25 October 1983. That result was matched by Liverpool against Fulham, also in the second round, on 23 September 1986.

16   West Ham United won a club-record 16 home league matches in succession between 30 August 1980 and 7 March 1981.

19   West Ham United lost a club-record 19 consecutive away matches between 28 November 1959 and 15 October 1960.

27   West Ham United have gone 27 league matches without failing to score a goal on two occasions – between 22 January and 15 October 1927 and between 5 October 1957 and 4 April 1958.

29   West Ham United conceded just 29 league goals during the 1980/81 Division Two promotion season, a club-record low.

50   Vic Watson scored 50 goals in all competitions in 1929/30, a club record.

101   West Ham United scored a club-record 101 goals in securing the Division Two title in 1957/58.

326   Vic Watson is West Ham United's all-time record goalscorer, netting 326 times in 505 appearances between 1920 and 1935.

793   Billy Bonds made a club-record 793 first-team appearances for West Ham United between 1967 and 1988.

1900   West Ham United was officially inaugurated in June 1900, five years after the club's predecessor, Thames Ironworks FC, had been founded.

42,322   A club-record 42,322 supporters watched West Ham United and Tottenham Hotspur draw 2-2 at the Boleyn Ground on 17 October 1970.

7,500,000   West Ham United paid a club-record £7,500,000 to sign Wales forward Craig Bellamy from Liverpool in July 2007.

18,000,000   The largest transfer fee West Ham United have ever received was the £18,000,000 Leeds United paid for England defender Rio Ferdinand in November 2000.

WEST HAM
UNITED
BY NUMBERS

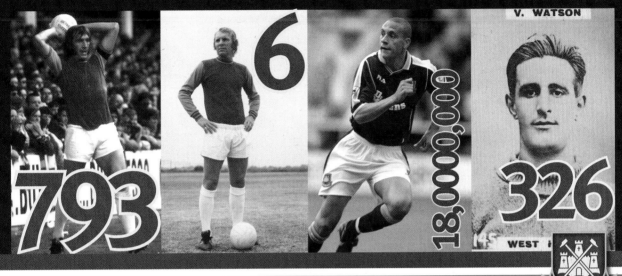

793

6

18,000,000

V. WATSON

326

WEST HAM UNITED

1

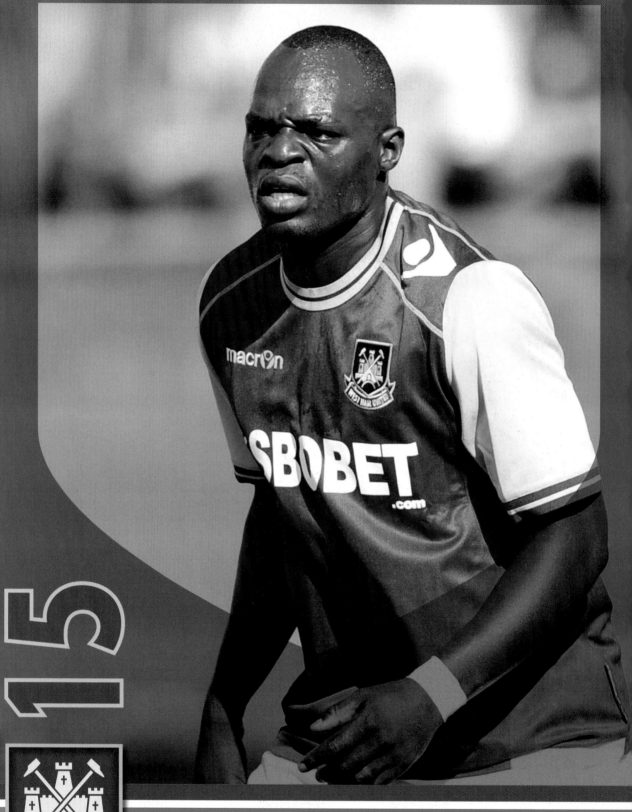

15

WEST HAM UNITED

ABDOULAYE
FAYE

QUIZ TIME

ANSWERS ON PAGE 58.

HAMMERS TEASERS

Can you answer the following West Ham United-related questions?

1. Which midfielder did West Ham United sign from Newcastle United in June 2011?

2. What was West Ham United FC called between 1895 and 1900?

3. What is West Ham United manager Sam Allardyce's nickname?

4. Which Academy graduate and former England Under-21 captain is West Ham United's longest-serving player?

5. What is the name of West Ham United's Academy home ground?

6. Which player, with 326 goals to his name, has scored more times for West Ham United than any other player?

7. Which player has made more appearances for West Ham United, 793, than any other?

8. Which three West Ham United players appeared for England in the 1966 FIFA World Cup final victory over West Germany?

9. Which player is wearing the No10 shirt for West Ham United during the 2011/12 season?

10. What is the correct name of West Ham United's stadium?

MISSING LINEUP

Fill in the gaps to complete the starting lineup in West Ham United's 4-0 Carling Cup fifth-round win over Manchester United on 30 November 2010.

_ _ _ _ _ _(6) _ _ _ _ _(5)

JULIEN FAUBERT

_ _ _ _ _(5) _ _ _ _ _ _ _(7)

_ _ _ _ _ _ _ (7) _ _ _ _ _(5)

_ _ (3) _ _ _ - _ _ _ _ (3-4)

_ _ _ _ _ _ (5) _ _ _ _ _ _ (7)

JONATHAN SPECTOR

_ _ _ _ _ _ _ (8) _ _ _ _ (5)

_ _ _ (4) _ _ _ - _ _ _ _ (3-5)

CARLTON COLE

_ _ _ _ _ _(6) _ _ _ _ _ _(6)

WHO IS THE HAMMER?

Who is the West Ham United player celebrating after scoring a goal?

ANAGRAMS

Can you work out the identities of the jumbled up West Ham United players' names?

1. Blank more

2. I conquered fine rip

3. Jokes man mist

4. Ya deaf able you

5. Malt Rat Toy

6. Bee Iron Joy

7. Jar Cow Hen

8. Lilac Jocks On

9. Barber Lap Oar

10. Bun Duo Riff

EAT LIKE A PROFESSIONAL

From the young schoolboys and scholars at Little Heath through to the senior first-teamers at Chadwell Heath, it is important that every West Ham United player looks after himself.

While daily training sessions and matches help them to maintain a high level of physical fitness, it is also imperative that players of all ages eat the right foods and drink the right drinks to continue to grow and develop.

Generally speaking, professional footballers avoid food with high fat content and stick to foods that are high in carbohydrates – which provide energy – and, to a lesser extent, proteins – which help to build and repair muscles.

To help you to eat like a professional, the Hammers' club chef Adam Viggars has put together a menu of dishes that will help you to lead a healthy lifestyle.

BREAKFAST
West Ham United's players usually eat breakfast around two hours before they begin training. However, whether you are training, playing or simply going to school, breakfast is an important meal as it provides energy for the day ahead and helps you to concentrate on the tasks in hand.

It is also important to take plenty of fluids on board to ensure you are properly hydrated before taking to the pitch for either training or a match.

So, to kick-off your day like a professional footballer, eat one of the following foods for your breakfast –

Breakfast cereal with skimmed milk

Toast or bread with jam or honey

Fresh fruit

Yoghurt

Orange juice, tea or coffee

LUNCH/PRE-MATCH MEAL
Your lunch or pre-match meal should be eaten three hours before kick-off and should be high in carbohydrates, which are the fuel that your body needs to perform at the highest level.

Your pre-match meal should be low in fat, protein and fibre, not be too bulky, and should be easy to digest.

Examples of lunches and pre-match meals eaten by West Ham United players include –

Spaghetti or another type of pasta with tomato sauce and small bread rolls

Grilled chicken breast with pasta

Grilled fish with rice or pasta

Boiled vegetables

Fresh fruit

DURING THE TRAINING SESSION/MATCH
Make sure you keep hydrated by drinking plenty of water and/or isotonic drinks during your training session or match.

You will lose fluids throughout the session or match through sweating and breathing heavily and it is essential that you replace these to help your body maintain its energy levels.

It is also important to drink plenty of water after the final whistle to replace fluids lost when you go to the toilet after the match has finished.

POST-MATCH
Your post-match meal is very important in helping your body to recover from the rigours of running around for 90 minutes.

As such, to replace lost nutrients – in particular the energy-storing molecule glycogen – players should eat and drink within an hour of the final whistle. Immediately after the match has finished, you should also consume a drink that is high in carbohydrates.

Food-wise, try some of the following foods as your post-match meal –

Grilled chicken breast and rice or pasta

Grilled fish and rice or pasta

Jacket potatoes

Sandwiches

Pizza

Fresh fruit

EAT LIKE A PROFESSIONAL

Grilled chicken breast and rice or pasta

Grilled fish and rice or pasta

Jacket potatoes

Sandwiches

Pizza

Fresh fruit

CAUGHT ON CAMERA

West Ham United line up for a photo call ahead of their meeting with Swiss champions FC Basel in Grenchen, Switzerland, on Wednesday 16 July 2011. Junior Stanislas was on target for the Hammers, only for their opponents to run out 2-1 winners.

BACK ROW: (left to right) Joey O'Brien, Frederic Piquionne, Kevin Nolan, James Tomkins, Winston Reid, Marek Stech.

FRONT ROW: (left to right) Jordan Spence, Herita Ilunga, Freddie Sears, Robert Hall, Junior Stanislas.

PRE-SEASON
TRAINING CAMP

West Ham United got down to work at their pre-season training camp in Switzerland.

The squad wait patiently to check-in ahead of their flight from London City Airport to Bern.

READY FOR THE OFF

The view from the team hotel the following morning was something truly special.

THE PERFECT START

Manager Sam Allardyce and his staff took the West Ham United squad for a six-day pre-season training camp in Switzerland in July 2011. The Hammers were based in the picturesque town of Spiez on the banks of Lake Thun, 30 miles south of the capital city Bern.

There, the players were put through their paces three times a day, taking part in a range of traditional fitness and football sessions as well as swimming, water polo, cycling and circuit training.

The trip also featured matches against Swiss Super League sides BSC Young Boys and FC Basel in the town of Grenchen, both of which ended in narrow 2-1 defeats.

West Ham United's training base in the town of Spiez was in beautiful surroundings.

TRAINING IN THE SUN

James Tomkins and Jack Collison were the victors in a thrilling mini-golf competition.

GOLFING GREATS

Frank Nouble scored the Hammers' goal in a 2-1 defeat by BSC Young Boys.

FRANK ON TARGET

PRE-SEASON
TRAINING CAMP

Jack Collison was the hero as his team won an exciting water polo competition.

WATER BABY JACK

Young forward Cristian Montano showed his prowess from the five-metre springboard.

CRISTIAN CAN FLY!

The central tower of nearby Spiez Castle dates from the 13th century.

Junior Stanislas scored a penalty in the 2-1 defeat by Swiss champions FC Basel.

JUNIOR ON THE SPOT

Carlton Cole demonstrated his basketball skills during a circuit training session.

CYCLING SAM

Manager Sam Allardyce joined the players in cycling the two miles to training each day.

DUNKING CARLTON

A TO Z
WEST HAM HEROES

A – MALCOLM ALLISON
Commonly considered to be the architect behind the club's Academy of Football youth development and training methods, Malcolm Allison made more than 250 first-team appearances over eight seasons before his playing career was cut short by tuberculosis. A talented coach, 'Big Mal' later enjoyed a successful spell as manager of Manchester City.

B – BILLY BONDS
A four-times Hammer of the Year who spent more than 20 years in the West Ham United first-team squad, Billy Bonds has made more appearances for the club than any other player – 793. A strong and committed central defender or midfielder, Bonds had rare leadership qualities and captained the Hammers to FA Cup success in 1975 and 1980.

C – TONY COTTEE
A diminutive and goal-hungry striker, Tony Cottee came through the Academy ranks before scoring on his debut at Tottenham Hotspur on New Year's Day 1983. Voted Hammer of the Year for the record-breaking 1985/86 season, Cottee netted 146 goals in 336 appearances over two spells at the Boleyn Ground and was capped seven times by England.

D – ALAN DEVONSHIRE
An elusive and skilful player, Alan Devonshire was snapped up from non-league Southall for a bargain fee of just £5,000 in 1976. The dashing, moustachioed midfielder repaid West Ham United's faith by being voted Hammer of the Year in 1979, winning the FA Cup in 1980 and making 448 first-team appearances, scoring 32 goals.

E – STAN EARLE
A forward, Stan Earle won the FA Amateur Cup with Clapton Orient in 1924 before joining West Ham United later the same year. Born in Stratford, Earle made a total of 273 appearances for the Hammers, scoring 58 goals. His talents also saw him capped by England at both amateur and senior level.

F – TED FENTON
A wing-half and manager, Ted Fenton served West Ham United on and off the pitch for 25 years. After joining the club as a schoolboy, Fenton made 383 appearances, scoring 63 goals. As manager, he won the Division Two title in 1958, reached two FA Youth Cup finals and paved the way for the glory days of the 1960s.

G – ERNIE GREGORY

One of the finest goalkeepers ever to pull on a West Ham United shirt, Ernie Gregory made 481 appearances for the club between 1946 and 1959. Born in Stratford and capped by England at B level, Gregory remained at the club following his retirement, coaching the reserves and the first team before finally hanging up his boots in 1987.

H – GEOFF HURST

Famous for scoring the only hat-trick in FIFA World Cup final history in England's 4-2 victory over West Germany in 1966, Geoff Hurst had already made his name as a prolific centre forward with West Ham United. The scorer of 249 goals in 502 appearances, Hurst won the FA Cup in 1964 and European Cup Winners' Cup a year later.

I – PAUL INCE

The 1988/89 Hammer of the Year, Paul Ince burst on to the scene in the late 1980s after coming through the Academy ranks. A combative all-round midfield player, Ince joined West Ham United at the age of 12 after being spotted by manager John Lyall. He was later capped 53 times by England.

J – BILLY JENNINGS

Born in Hackney, Billy Jennings joined West Ham United from Watford in 1974, helping the club to lift the FA Cup in his first season at the club. The following season, 1975/76, forward Jennings was on target regularly as the Hammers reached the European Cup Winners' Cup final.

K – GEORGE KAY

Centre-back George Kay was West Ham United's captain in the famous 'White Horse' FA Cup final against Bolton Wanderers in 1923. After serving in the Royal Artillery during the First World War, Kay became the first player to make 200 Football League appearances for the Hammers and later managed Liverpool for 15 years.

L – FRANK LAMPARD

East Ham-born Frank Lampard is a true West Ham United great. A left-back, Lampard made his first-team debut in November 1967 and went on to make 551 appearances over the next 18 years. Capped twice by England, he won two FA Cups and the Division Two title before later returning to the club as assistant manager to Harry Redknapp.

M – BOBBY MOORE

The incomparable Bobby Moore was, quite simply, the finest player in West Ham United's history. A centre-back blessed with immaculate tackling ability and an unrivalled reading of the game, Moore captained the Hammers to FA Cup and European Cup Winners' Cup success before leading England to FIFA World Cup glory in 1966.

N – LUCAS NEILL

Australia captain Lucas Neill joined West Ham United in January 2007 with the club in dire straits at the bottom of the Premier League table. An inspirational leader, Neill helped the Hammers to steer clear of relegation in dramatic style before skippering the club to consecutive top-half finishes.

O – FRANK O'FARRELL

A Republic of Ireland international wing-half, Frank O'Farrell joined West Ham United from Cork United in January 1948. A determined but quietly-spoken individual, O'Farrell forced his way into the starting XI and went on to make more than 200 appearances before joining Preston North End in 1956 and later managing Manchester United.

P – SYD PUDDEFOOT

A truly prolific centre forward, Syd Puddefoot scored more than 200 goals for the club, netting in the Southern League, War-time London Combination and Football League between 1913 and 1922. Born in Bow, Puddefoot represented Falkirk, Blackburn Rovers and England before returning to Hammers for a short second spell in 1932.

Q – JIMMY QUINN

One of just four players with a surname beginning with the letter 'Q' to represent West Ham United, Jimmy Quinn was a Northern Ireland international striker who spent two seasons with the club between 1989 and 1991. During that period, Quinn netted 22 goals in 57 appearances in all competitions before joining Bournemouth.

R – JIMMY RUFFELL

A talented left winger, Jimmy Ruffell made more than 500 first-team appearances for West Ham United between 1921 and 1937. The club's top scorer on two occasions, Ruffell netted 148 goals for the club and was part of the side that contested the famous 1923 'White Horse' FA Cup final against Bolton Wanderers at Wembley.

S – DANNY SHEA

One of West Ham United's first real star players, Danny Shea was born in Wapping and spotted playing pub football by Hammers manager Charlie Paynter in 1907. Shea was the club's leading scorer in five consecutive seasons between 1908 and 1912 before joining Blackburn Rovers for a record £2,000 fee.

T – ALAN TAYLOR

Alan Taylor will forever be remembered as the man who scored both West Ham United goals in their 2-0 FA Cup final win over Fulham at Wembley in May 1975. Signed from Rochdale for £40,000 the previous year, Taylor also netted in the quarter-final and semi-final victories over Arsenal and Ipswich Town.

U – MATTHEW UPSON

Former West Ham United captain Matthew Upson joined the club in January 2007, only to miss out on the 'Great Escape' from relegation from the Premier League due to a recurring calf injury. Upson returned to form and fitness in time to score for England against Germany at the 2010 FIFA World Cup in South Africa.

V – FRANCOIS VAN DER ELST

Belgium international Francois van der Elst quickly established himself as a fans' favourite after joining West Ham United from New York Cosmos in 1981. Previously, Van der Elst had been part of the RSC Anderlecht squad that beat the Hammers in the 1976 European Cup Winners' Cup final, while he also appeared at the 1982 FIFA World Cup.

W – VIC WATSON

West Ham United's all-time leading scorer was, amazingly, signed for just £50 from non-league club Wellingborough in 1920. Over the next 15 years, the Cambridgeshire-born forward netted an incredible 326 goals, including six in an 8-2 victory over Leeds United in February 1929. He also scored four times in five appearances for England.

Y – TOMMY YEWS

Born in County Durham, talented winger Tommy Yews joined West Ham United from Hartlepool United for a £150 fee in 1923. Playing alongside the likes of Jimmy Ruffell and Vic Watson, Yews flourished, scoring 51 goals in 361 appearances for the club before leaving for Clapton Orient in 1933.

Z – BOBBY ZAMORA

Born in Barking, Bobby Zamora made his name as a prolific striker with Brighton & Hove Albion before enjoying a productive four-and-a-half year stay with West Ham United. A complete forward, Zamora was instrumental in the club's escape from relegation in 2006/07 and went on to appear for England after joining Fulham in July 2008.

It's time to show you have great taste by baking some West Ham United cupcakes

Ask an adult to help you to bake your West Ham United cupcakes.

This recipe should take about half-an-hour and make 12 cupcakes for you to enjoy with your family, friends or fellow Hammers!

BAKE CLARET & BLUE CUPCAKES!

BAKING YOUR CUPCAKES

OK, now it's time to start baking!

Follow the recipe step by step, being careful to ensure you get the measurements and temperatures right.

1. Preheat your electric oven to 180C (160C if you have a fan oven) or Gas Mark Four and place 12 paper cases on to a baking tray.

2. Using a whisk, food processor or wooden spoon, beat the butter and sugar until very light and fluffy.

3. Add the eggs one at a time, beating each one in well before adding the next. Add the vanilla essence.

4. Carefully fold in the flour and baking powder.

5. Alternatively, you can mix the ingredients together using a food processor. Use the pulse button to mix together in between adding the ingredients in the order above.

6. Bake in the oven for ten to 20 minutes. After ten minutes, check to see if the cupcakes are ready by inserting a cocktail stick into one of the cupcakes. If it comes out dry then the cupcakes are done. If not, then put them back in the oven for a few minutes more. Don't overcook the cupcakes otherwise they will dry out.

7. Take the cupcakes out of the oven and off the backing tray and leave them to cool on a wire rack.

8. For a claret and blue icing topping, add a little water to some icing sugar until you have a smooth paste. When they have cooled, squeeze some icing mixture on top to decorate your cupcakes in West Ham United colours!

9. Try drawing West Ham United-related patterns on your cupcakes. For example, you could draw the crossed hammers, a football or football boot or even try to write the club's name!

COLOUR IN
THE HAMMER

Can you copy the image of Mark Noble on the opposite page to give the West Ham United midfielder his claret and blue colours back?

Jordan Spence explains how football is a job that cannot be taken lightly. If you think that professional footballers simply turn up on a Saturday afternoon to play for 90 minutes, think again!

The demands of modern-day football mean players have to think about their careers 24/7 – whether they are at the training ground, stadium or simply resting at home.

Defender Jordan Spence takes you through a week as a West Ham United player.

MONDAY

The day before a game is usually the same, whether it be a Tuesday game, a Saturday game or a Sunday game.

We will have a light training session and I imagine that we will also go through some sort of team shape and make ourselves aware of the opposition. Training will have in mind the team we're going to be playing against.

It's normally quite short and quite sharp the day before a game.

We always make ourselves aware of the strengths and weaknesses of our opponents, all the way down to their set pieces and areas we can exploit with our own strengths.

We will be made aware of these on video and verbally as well. We get a personal DVD of our own individual performance after each game and, if I want to do some research on a wide player or a centre forward, I can ask for one to be made and sit down and watch that.

I'll go to bed early.

TUESDAY

I just try to keep my routine on a matchday the same as all my other days. I treat matches as an extension of training and try to keep everything the same. I try to not make it any more different than it needs to be.

During the day, the boys will have different routines. Some will sleep up until the time they leave home, while I treat it like a normal day.

I get up as I find if I stay in bed I'll be a little bit lethargic, so I get up and do some normal things.

We get into the ground about four hours before kick-off and eat a pre-match meal three hours before the game.

We eat something with lots of carbohydrates and a bit of protein in it – maybe some fish or chicken. I only eat a moderate amount because I don't want to feel too heavy, but you have to take enough on board to get you through because it's quite a long wait from the meal to the game itself.

Normally, we'll go out and do our warm-up on the pitch and we won't be given too much information, because we will have prepared fully for the game in the days before.

We will be made aware of the set pieces again because they're a massive thing, then we'll have a final word and be ready.

After the game, we eat straight away. It's normally easier to get something down you and fuel up if you've won!

If we've played well, we might also have to fulfil media commitments for the club, radio stations and television channels. It's all part of the job!

WEDNESDAY

I'd normally plump for a day off, but recovery and getting your body right are vital when you are playing two games a week, so you'll quite often come in on a Wednesday or a Sunday just to do something to keep myself on the mood and aid the recovery process.

We may also be called upon to fulfil community commitments, which can be anything from holding a training session with children to meeting you, the supporters, for a signing session at one of the Club Stores.

THURSDAY

I call Thursday my 'Work day' as you have nothing straight before it and nothing straight after it in terms of matches.

You can get out and train for a little bit longer, do some extras and spend the afternoon in the gym. You can do stuff on a Thursday that you can't do on a Friday or on any other day.

FRIDAY

If we are playing a fair distance away, we normally train and then travel up to the hotel on the afternoon before the game.

It's all about settling in and relaxing and making sure you do things right.

A WEEK IN THE LIFE OF A FOOTBALLER

Our training programmes are roughly the same, but obviously everybody has specific individual needs and their itineraries can be quite different.

I tend to take out a book or a box set and just relax in my room, while quite a lot of the other lads will have a massage and get themselves stretched out. Others you won't see that often. It depends on each individual player.

SATURDAY

For an away match on a Saturday, we'll usually have breakfast together at the hotel and we might go out for a walk to loosen the limbs before relaxing and maybe having a short sleep.

As on Tuesday, we will eat three hours before kick-off and we arrive at the stadium around 90 minutes before the game starts.

The match routine is the same for home and away games, but obviously we will have to travel home after the away matches.

SUNDAY

Sunday is a rest day and one for you to spend with your family, unless you have a match on the following Tuesday, in which case we will be called in for a short session to help us to recover.

If we don't have a midweek match, then it's a welcome day to spend at home.

All in all, we are involved in a job that is seven-days-a-week and even when you have a break, you are watching what you are eating and what you are doing and generally taking care of yourself.

The sacrifices are all worthwhile though when you play for a club like West Ham United.

West Ham United was founded in 1895 as Thames Ironworks FC before being reformed in 1900. In 1904 the club relocated to their current Boleyn Ground stadium in Upton Park.

After initially competing in the Southern League and Western League, West Ham joined the Football League in 1919. Four years later, the Hammers celebrated the twin achievements of gaining promotion to Division One and reaching the first-ever Wembley FA Cup final, where they were beaten by Bolton Wanderers.

In 1940 the team won the inaugural Football League War Cup, defeating Blackburn Rovers at Wembley.

West Ham have continued to be regular visitors to the Home of Football, winning the FA Cup in 1964, 1975 and 1980 and the European Cup Winners' Cup in 1965, defeating German side TSV 1860 Munich 2-0 in the final.

The Hammers have also reached Wembley in the League Cup, holding Liverpool to a draw in 1981 before being beaten in a replay at Villa Park.

The club also finished as runners-up to West Bromwich Albion in the same competition in 1966 – the same year in which Bobby Moore, Geoff Hurst and Martin Peters led England to FIFA World Cup glory.

In continental competition, aside from their 1965 triumph, the Hammers reached the final of the European Cup Winners' Cup again in 1976, losing to Belgian club RSC Anderlecht, and won the UEFA Intertoto Cup in 1999.

In terms of league position, West Ham's highest-ever finish was the third place achieved by John Lyall's squad in 1985/86.

Unfortunately for the club, those past glories meant nothing as they were relegated from the Premier League after a six-year stay in the top-flight in May 2011.

West Ham supporters will hope the appointment of Sam Allardyce as the club's 14th full-time manager and the signing of former Newcastle United midfielder Kevin Nolan will signal an upturn in their fortunes.

WEST HAM UNITED
A HISTORY

A concise look back on the history of the Hammers.

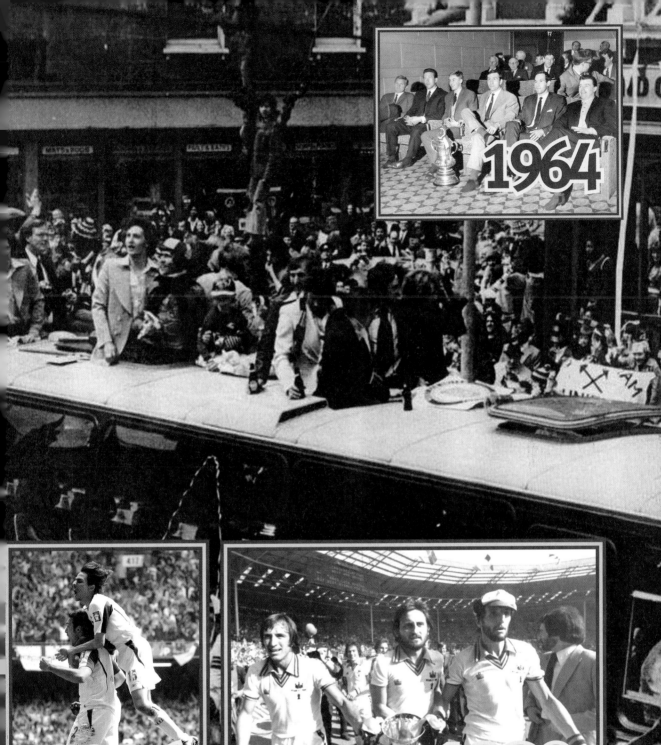

1964

2006

1980

WEST HAM UNITED

AUSTRALIA

Youth-team striker DYLAN TOMBIDES was born in Perth in Western Australia, voted the eighth-best city to live in the world. Tombides appeared for Australia at the 2011 FIFA Under-17 World Cup finals.

BELGIUM

RUUD BOFFIN hails from the town of Sint-Truiden in the Flemish region of Belgium, which is famous for being the centre of the country's fruit-growing industry. Boffin has been capped at youth level.

CZECH REPUBLIC

Czech Republic Under-21 internatioanal goalkeeper MAREK STECH hails from Prague, the capital city that was once the capital of the Holy Roman Empire and is the sixth most-visited city in Europe.

DR CONGO

The city of Kinshasa, where HERITA ILUNGA was born and raised, was once a tiny fishing village but it is now home to an estimated ten million inhabitants and is capital of the Democratic Republic of Congo.

FRANCE

The city of Le Havre, where France international JULIEN FAUBERT was born, is situated at the mouth of the River Seine, which famously runs all the way south into the capital city of Paris.

HUNGARY

Hungary Under-21 international goalkeeper PETER KURUCZ was born in the historical capital city Budapest, which is actually comprised of two towns on opposite banks of the River Danube – Buda and Pest!

MEXICO

PABLO BARRERA hails from the city of Tlalnepantla de Baz, which was founded in the 11th century by the Amaquemecan people. It is now home to more than 650,000 inhabitants.

West Ham United players are drawn from all over the planet.

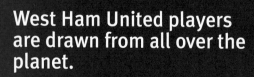

HAMMERS ALL OVER THE WORLD

NEW CALEDONIA

The nation of New Caledonia, where FREDERIC PIQUIONNE was born in the capital city of Noumea, is comprised of the main island Grande Terre, the Loyalty Islands, and several smaller islands.

NEW ZEALAND

North Shore, which is where New Zealand international WINSTON REID was born, was a city in its own right before being amalgamated into the larger city of Auckland in 2010.

NORTHERN IRELAND

Belfast, the capital city of Northern Ireland and birthplace of GEORGE McCARTNEY, was where the ill-fated ocean liner RMS Titanic was built by Harland and Wolff in the early 20th century.

NORWAY

Oslo, where Norway international striker JOHN CAREW was born, is officially the second most-expensive city in the world behind the Japanese capital Tokyo.

REPUBLIC OF IRELAND

The name of Dublin in Irish is derived from the Irish name Dubh Linn, meaning 'Black Pool'. Dublin is also the birthplace of Republic of Ireland international JOEY O'BRIEN.

SENEGAL

Dakar, the capital city of Senegal and the birthplace of defender ABDOULAYE FAYE, is famous for being the westernmost city on the continent of Africa.

West Ham United have a host of promising young players hoping to make their mark.

Ever since West Ham United were formed in 1900, the club has focused on bringing through the very best young players.

In the late 1950s, that commitment came to fruition as the 'Academy of Football' was formed under the watchful eye of manager Ted Fenton and senior player Malcolm Allison.

The likes of Bobby Moore, Geoff Hurst, Martin Peters and many more began a production line that has seen the Hammers produce dozens of top-class footballers.

In more recent decades, the likes of Trevor Brooking, Tony Cottee, Frank Lampard and Rio Ferdinand have ensured the club retains its reputation as one of the best producers of talent anywhere in world football.

This season, the likes of Mark Noble, Jack Collison and James Tomkins are set to play an important role in the club's challenge for promotion.

Lower down the age-scale, the development squad and Academy is crammed full of aspiring youngsters who are striving to following in the footsteps of their illustrious predecessors.

Among them are five possible stars of tomorrow – Cristian Montano, George Moncur, Robert Hall, Blair Turgott and Elliot Lee.

CRISTIAN MONTANO

BORN: 11 December 1991, Cali, Colombia
POSITION: Forward/Left winger

GEORGE MONCUR

BORN: 18 August 1993, London, England
POSITION: Central midfielder

The 2009/10 Academy Player of the Year, Cristian Montano continued his development last season before making a real impact during the build-up to the 2011/12 campaign.

Born in Colombia, Montano joined the first-team squad at their pre-season training camp in Switzerland, catching the eye in fixtures against BSC Young Boys and FC Basel.

Montano continued to impress in the club's other pre-season matches, setting up a late winner for Freddie Sears against Danish champions FC Copenhagen.

The South American moved to Notts County on loan in August 2011, making his senior debut in a Carling Cup first-round tie against Nottingham Forest the same month.

Now a first-year professional, George Moncur has long been considered one of West Ham United's brightest young prospects.

The son of former Hammers midfielder John Moncur, the younger Moncur is blessed with fine technique, a good passing range and is deadly from set-plays.

A hard-working player, Moncur was a regular starter for West Ham's reserve team in 2010/11 and is eyeing a first-team debut at some stage this season.

Still only 18, the youngster has been capped by England at Under-18 level and joined the Hammers on their first-team training camp in Switzerland in summer 2011.

COMING THROUGH
THE RANKS

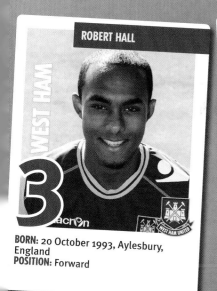

ROBERT HALL

BORN: 20 October 1993, Aylesbury, England
POSITION: Forward

BLAIR TURGOTT

BORN: 22 May 1994, London, England
POSITION: Midfielder

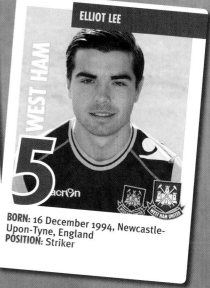

ELLIOT LEE

BORN: 16 December 1994, Newcastle-Upon-Tyne, England
POSITION: Striker

That Robert Hall was disappointed to score ten goals in 26 youth-team appearances in 2010/11 says much for the young striker's high expectations.

A UEFA European Under-17 Championship winner with England in 2010, Hall has now been capped at Under-18 level and has often been called upon to train with the Hammers' first-team squad.

Hall, who signed his first professional contract with the club in October 2010, is blessed with great pace, ability to run with the ball and beat his opponent and a sharp eye for goal.

Blessed with a strong will-to-win, Hall will be eager to make his mark at senior level before too long.

Blair Turgott enjoyed a fantastic 2011, appearing for England at the UEFA European Under-17 Championship and the FIFA Under-17 World Cup before returning to sign his first professional contract with West Ham United.

The midfielder is capable of playing in a variety of positions, but favours a position on the right or left wing, where he utilises his pace and elusive running to get past opponents with ease.

Turgott is also blessed with a rocket-like shot from long range, which he has shown to good effect at both domestic and international level.

Still only 17, Turgott has plenty of time to turn his immense promise into a successful senior career.

A striker with an unerring eye for goal and strength and pace in the mould of a young Wayne Rooney, Elliot Lee is considered to be one of West Ham United's brightest prospects.

The son of former Hammers and England midfielder Rob Lee and the younger brother of midfielder Olly, the teenager has scored bucket-loads of goals at all age-group levels on his way through the Academy.

After making his debut for the reserves in early 2011, Lee ended the season with a match-winning youth-team hat-trick against Chelsea.

Should he continue to work hard, Lee has every chance of following his father by playing at the highest level.

A TO Z OF WEST HAM UNITED

A – ACADEMY OF FOOTBALL

The Academy of Football is a nickname given to West Ham United's successful youth department, which has produced more than 20 full internationals since being instigated by manager Ted Fenton and player Malcolm Allison in the late 1950s. The Academy met regularly at Cassettari's Café in Barking Road to discuss tactics, nutrition and other important issues.

B – BUBBLES

Written by John Kellette, the song 'I'm Forever Blowing Bubbles' debuted in the Broadway musical The Passing Show of 1918. The tune was introduced to West Ham United by manager Charlie Paynter in the late 1920s because a player like Billy 'Bubbles' Murray looked like the boy in the famous 'Bubbles' painting by Millais used in a Pears soap commercial of the time, with the fans starting to sing the song before home matches soon afterwards.

C – CLARET AND BLUE

Thames Ironworks FC first wore claret and blue colours in 1899, reportedly after right-half Charlie Dove received the Aston Villa kit from his father William Dove, a sprinter who won the strip in a race against one of Villa's players. This version of events is disputed, but Thames Ironworks and later West Ham United retained the colours.

D – DEAR

Striker Brian Dear set a British football record when he scored five goals in the space of 20 minutes either side of half-time in West Ham United's 6-1 Division One win over West Bromwich Albion on 16 April 1965. Aged just 21, Plaistow-born Dear also started the Hammers' European Cup Winners' Cup final win over TSV 1860 Munich at Wembley the following month.

E – EAST HAM

Despite the club's name, West Ham United is actually situated on the western edge of the district of East Ham within the London Borough of Newham. Now a multi-cultural area, East Ham is home to a London Underground station of the same name, as well as Flanders Playing Fields, where a young Bobby Moore first started playing football.

F – FA CUP

West Ham United have won the FA Cup on three occasions, defeating Preston North End 3-2 in 1964, Fulham 2-0 in 1975 and Arsenal 1-0 in 1980. The Hammers' 1980 success makes them the last Division Two side to lift the trophy. In all, West Ham have contested 306 FA Cup ties, winning 129, drawing 84 and losing 93.

G – GORNIK ZABRZE

West Ham United took on Polish side Gornik Zabrze in the Championship match at the 1963 International Soccer League in the United States. The Hammers finished top of their group ahead of AC Mantova, Kilmarnock, Sport Recife, Preussen Munster, Deportivo Oro and Valenciennes FC before being defeated 2-1 on aggregate by Gornik Zabrze in the final.

H – HERMIT ROAD

Hermit Road in Canning Town was the first home stadium occupied by Thames Ironworks FC, the club that would become West Ham United. Thames Ironworks took over the ground from Old Castle Swifts FC in 1895, drawing 0-0 with Royal Ordnance in their first fixture there on 7 September of that year. The club moved on to Browning Road in early 1897.

I – INTERNATIONAL MATCHES

The Boleyn Ground has played host to two full international matches. Wayne Rooney made his England debut in a 3-1 friendly defeat by Australia on 12 February 2003, while Mario Balotelli did likewise for Italy in their 1-0 friendly defeat by Ivory Coast on 10 August 2010. The stadium has also hosted women's and age-group international fixtures.

J – JOKERIT

West Ham United beat Finnish side FC Jokerit 2-1 on aggregate on their way to winning the UEFA Intertoto Cup in the summer of 1999. Having overcome Jokerit, the Hammers defeated Dutch club SC Heerenveen 2-0 and French outfit FC Metz 3-2 to qualify for the UEFA Cup. There, West Ham overcame Croatian side NK Osijek before being knocked out by Romanians Steaua Bucharest.

K – KING

Syd King played for both Thames Ironworks FC and West Ham United before embarking on a successful management career with the Hammers. King was in charge of team affairs between 1901 and 1932, overseeing the club's election to the Football League in 1919, led them to the FA Cup final and promotion to Division One in 1923.

L – LINCOLN CITY

Lincoln City provided West Ham United's first-ever Football League opposition on 30 August 1919. The Imps held the Hammers to a 1-1 Division Two draw at the Boleyn Ground, with James Moyes having the honour of scoring the club's inaugural Football League goal. A crowd of 20,000 spectators turned out to watch the historic match.

D

F

G

J

I

K

M – MEMORIAL GROUNDS

The Memorial Grounds were the home of Thames Ironworks FC and West Ham United for seven seasons between 1897 and 1904, when the club moved to the Boleyn Ground. The Memorial Grounds opened in June 1897 to celebrate Queen Victoria's diamond jubilee. Thames Ironworks defeated Brentford 1-0 in the London League on 11 September in their first match at their new home.

N – NATIONALITIES

West Ham United's squad for the 2011/12 season contained players of 14 different nationalities – Australian, Belgian, Congolese, Czech, English, French, Hungarian, Irish, Mexican, New Zealander, Northern Irish, Norwegian, Senegalese and Welsh. In the past, the club has been represented by players from all over the world, including Cameroon, Canada, Guinea, Italy, Netherlands, Romania and the United States.

O – OLYMPIC STADIUM

West Ham United plan to move into the London 2012 Olympic Stadium in Stratford in summer 2014. The stadium will continue to house a running track and will host a number of different sporting and popular culture events, with plans to hold athletics, cricket, American football, pop concerts and community events at the 60,000-capacity stadium.

P – PLAY-OFFS

West Ham United have taken part in the end-of-season Football League Championship Play-Offs on two occasions. In 2004/05, the Hammers defeated Ipswich Town 2-1 on aggregate before losing 1-0 to Crystal Palace in the final. The following season, 2005/06, West Ham overcame Ipswich 4-2 on aggregate in the semi-finals before defeating Preston North End 1-0 in the final at the Millennium Stadium.

Q – QUEEN

HM Queen Elizabeth II and the Duke of Edinburgh paid a welcome visit to the Boleyn Ground in May 2002, when the monarch officially opened the new West Stand. The unveiling was one of a number of special events the Queen undertook as part of her golden jubilee celebrations. Following the opening of the new stand, the illustrious couple were treated to a special luncheon by the club.

R – REAL MADRID CF

West Ham United took on the mighty Real Madrid CF in the American city of Houston on 20 April 1967. The fixture took place at the newly-completed Astrodome stadium, with Geoff Hurst and John Sissons scoring the Hammers' goals in a 3-2 defeat. Bobby Moore and Harry Redknapp also started the game against the six-times and reigning European Cup winners.

S – STATUE

The Champions statue is the famous bronze sculpture situated on the corner of Green Street and Barking Road. Philip Jackson's 4m-high memorial depicts West Ham United heroes Bobby Moore, Geoff Hurst and Martin Peters, along with England team-mate Ray Wilson, following their 1966 FIFA World Cup final victory over West Germany.

T – THAMES IRONWORKS FC

Thames Ironworks FC was founded by Thames Ironworks and Shipbuilding Co. Ltd owner Arnold Hills and foreman Dave Taylor in 1895. The club was in existence for five years, playing Southern League matches at Hermit Road, Browning Road and the Memorial Grounds before being dissolved in 1900 and re-launched as West Ham United FC.

U – UNDERGROUND

Most West Ham United and away supporters travelling by Tube travel to the Boleyn Ground by using Upton Park London Underground station. Opened in 1877 as part of the London, Tilbury and Southend Railway, the station is now served by the District, Hammersmith and City and Metropolitan lines.

V – VICTORIES

In the three major domestic competitions – Football and Premier League, FA Cup and League Cup – West Ham United had recorded 1,558 victories in the 4,029 matches the club had contested up until the start of the 2011/12 season. The Hammers had pulled off 1,328 league victories, 129 FA Cup wins and 101 League Cup wins before the current campaign.

W – WEMBLEY

West Ham United have played at Wembley on nine occasions – four FA Cup finals, one League Cup final, two Charity Shield matches, one European Cup Winners' Cup final and the Football League War Cup final. Of those matches, the Hammers have won five – three FA Cup finals, the 1965 European Cup Winners' Cup and the 1940 War Cup – drawn one and lost three.

Y – YOUTH CUP

West Ham United have won the FA Youth Cup on three occasions and been runners-up four times. The Hammers lifted the trophy in 1963, beating Liverpool 6-5 on aggregate, 1981, beating Tottenham Hotspur 2-1 on aggregate and 1999, when Coventry City were beaten 9-0 over two legs. West Ham were losing finalists in the competition in 1957, 1959, 1975 and 1996.

Z - ZIMBABWE

West Ham United visited what is modern-day Zimbabwe for a pre-season tour in 1962. The Hammers defeated Southern Rhodesia 5-0 and 3-0 in two challenge matches as part of a five-match trip that also saw the squad visit Nyasaland – now Malawi – and Ghana, where they defeated Asante Kotoko 4-0 and drew 1-1 with the Real Republicans.

COCA-COLA CHAMPIONSHIP PLAY OFF WINNERS 200
WEST HAM UNITED F.C.

QUIZ ANSWERS

HAMMERS TEASERS

1. Kevin Nolan
2. Thames Ironworks FC
3. 'Big Sam'
4. Mark Noble
5. Little Heath
6. Vic Watson
7. Billy Bonds
8. Bobby Moore, Geoff Hurst and Martin Peters
9. Jack Collison
10. The Boleyn Ground

WHO IS THE HAMMER?

Jack Collison

MISSING LINEUP

ROBERT GREEN
JULIEN FAUBERT
JAMES TOMKINS
MATTHEW UPSON
TAL BEN-HAIM
PABLO BARRERA
JONATHAN SPECTOR
RADOSLAV KOVAC
LUIS BOA-MORTE
CARLTON COLE
VICTOR OBINNA

ANAGRAMS

1. Mark Noble
2. Frederic Piquonne
3. James Tomkins
4. Abdoulaye Faye
5. Matt Taylor
6. Joey O'Brien
7. John Carew
8. Jack Collison
9. Pablo Barrera
10. Ruud Boffin

SPOT THE DIFFERENCE

14

WEST HAM UNITED

MATT TAYLOR

2012 CALENDAR

JANUARY

5	Cheye Alexander (17)
11	Jake Larkins (18)
15	David Gold (75)
18	Robert Green (32)
19	Jack Powell (18)
28	Marek Stech (22)
	Matthias Fanimo (18)

FEBRUARY

1	David Sullivan (63)
3	Nigel Seidu (17)
17	Joey O'Brien (26)
25	Herita Ilunga (30)
26	Abdoulaye Faye (34)

MARCH

8	Dylan Tombides (18)
29	James Tomkins (23)

APRIL

6	David Wootton (18)
13	Danny Potts (18)

MAY

8	Mark Noble (25)
18	Gary O'Neil (29)
22	Blair Turgott (18)
24	Jordan Spence (22)
30	Peter Kurucz (24)

JUNE

9	Wally Downes (51)
21	Pablo Barrera (25)
24	Kevin Nolan (30)

OCTOBER

MAY

JUNE

Like you, West Ham United's owners, players and management team will all celebrate a birthday in 2012!

JULY

3	Winston Reid (24)
11	Olly Lee (21)
	Taylor Miles (17)
28	Paul McCallum (19)

AUGUST

1	Julien Faubert (29)
5	Leo Chambers (17)
18	George Moncur (19)
24	Frank Nouble (21)

SEPTEMBER

5	Tony Carr (62)
6	John Carew (33)
8	Martyn Margetson (41)
14	Kieran Sadlier (18)
20	Sergio Sanchez (20)
21	Kenzer Lee (19)
23	Declan Hunt (19)
26	Matt Fry (22)

OCTOBER

2	Jack Collison (24)
	Eoin Wearen (20)
7	Dominic Siafa (18)
11	Jordan Brown (21)
	Sam Baxter (18)
13	Scott Parker (32)
14	Lamarr Hurley (19)
19	Sam Allardyce (57)
20	Robert Hall (19)
23	Callum Driver (20)
25	Callum McNaughton (21)
26	Sam Cowler (20)

NOVEMBER

2	Neil McDonald (47)
5	Ruud Boffin (25)
12	Carlton Cole (29)
	Ahmed Abdulla (21)
22	Dymon Labonne (18)
23	Dominic Vose (19)
26	Junior Stanislas (23)
27	Freddie Sears (23)
	Matt Taylor (31)

DECEMBER

5	Ian Hendon (41)
8	Frederic Piquionne (34)
11	Cristian Montano (21)
13	Jake Young (19)
16	Elliot Lee (18)
23	Frazer Shaw (18)
27	Zavon Hines (24)

JULY

NOVEMBER

OCTOBER

WHERE'S HERBIE?